Hope Was Heard Singing

Hope Was Heard Singing

Resources for Advent

Sally Foster-Fulton

wild goose
publications

www.ionabooks.com

Overseas distribution
Australia: Willow Connection Pty Ltd, Unit 4A, 3-9 Kenneth Road,
Manly Vale, NSW 2093
New Zealand: Pleroma, Higginson Street, Otane 4170, Central Hawkes Bay
Canada: Novalis/Bayard Publishing & Distribution, 10 Lower Spadina Ave.,
Suite 400, Toronto, Ontario M5V 2Z2

Printed by Bell & Bain, Thornliebank, Glasgow

MIX
Paper from
responsible sources
FSC
www.fsc.org   FSC® C007785

Contents

On light

On gifts

On prophets and heralds

On Christmas Eve

Introduction

The story we are waiting for tells itself over and over again – its advent a continuous circle. Love, life, birth …

Rather than offer a chronological countdown to Christmas, this book is a collection of reflections, prayers, poems, and a few wee plays thrown in for good measure. It's a book for dipping into. The themes gather round those evocative images that have taken up residence in the imagination of the story itself … images so profound as to live in collective memory. But while they do not live only in the Christmas story, they find a resonance there that magnifies them. Advent embodies expectation: that holding-of-the-breath forever-waiting for what has already begun …

There are so many people who helped me find the space to put this collection together. Thanks to my family for letting me type instead of helping with the tea, for listening to the same sentence in twenty different incarnations and for loving me when I wasn't being particularly likeable. Stuart, Alex and Gracie – thank you! (Mom and Dad did their fair share of e-mail editing too!)

To my good friends Frances Ann and Ruth and Glendon, who always give good advice and help keep things in perspective; and to my colleague and confidant Colin, whose friendship and support is constant and whose wonderful creativity is contagious. Finally, thank you to the church family at Dunblane Cathedral, who've heard almost all of these reflections before and seemed to like them.

Sally Foster-Fulton

WELCOME TO ADVENT

Bible readings

Psalm 25:1–10
Psalm 85
Isaiah 2:1–5
Isaiah 7:14
Mark 1:1–12
Mark 13:33–37
Luke 1:46–56
John 1:6–9
Romans 13:11–14
Romans 15:12–13

Come and do your will

Pride-scatterer, throne-toppler,
come and do your will.
Find our thoughts and challenge them,
open our minds and change them,
fill us with good things and
empty us fully.
For we know that nothing is impossible with you.

Now help us want nothing more
than a chance to be a part of your
kingdom coming.

What does Advent have to say?

What does Advent have to say to a post-religious society? How can we help people live in today's world? What do we have to offer?

Well, how about?: *Turn around, come back; wash away the dirt from the road that covers you with a dusty film, and begin again.*

How about?: *Come and join us on a journey* – because that is what life is and we need each other as we travel.

Jesus calls us to live life – and to live it abundantly … So, does that mean he who dies with the most toys wins? Or is there another way, if we are willing to help prepare it?

Trespassing God

God who tramps the highways of the world,
trespass now into the territory we covet.
Come and call us to your far-flung places:
where steadfast love and faithfulness meet;
where righteousness and peace kiss each other …
Our spirits long to go there with you,
our hearts are desperate to stay;
but the journey is long …

God who travels beside us,
hold our hearts and our hands,
and lead us on.

Turning point

Leader: Turn around, make a change. There is no better time.

People: The time is now.

Leader: Turn around. Do things differently. It's never too late to make things right.

People: The time is now.

Leader: The earth spins, hearts beat, seasons change – so do people.

People: So turn around, make a change. There is no better time.

Leader: The time is now.

ON WAITING

Bible readings

Psalm 40:1–5
Psalm 130
Isaiah 11:1–10
Isaiah 40:31
Matthew 3
Matthew 11:2–6
Luke 15:11–24
1 Corinthians 1:3–9

I will wait

I will wait … for you
To catch up
To tell me the truth
To challenge my lies …
I will wait for you.

I will wait … on you
Clear the dishes
Dry your tears
Sit beside you, and gently rub the back of your hand:
an invitation to take mine
and be held …
I will wait on you.

I will wait … with you
For the news you've been dreading
For the light to dawn
For forgiveness to find its way into your heart …
I will wait with you.

Remember who we're waiting for ...

At the advent of Advent, it's worth remembering who we're waiting for ... not a child in a manger, all swaddling clothes and innocence, but a man on a mission – with an uncompromising agenda – one that gives the whole world to the meek; one that asks us to give up all that the world tells us is important; one that says that true power can be found housed in the frailty of forgiveness, the virtue of vulnerability – that says there is freedom in saddling ourselves to the needs of others. We are waiting for a rebel. So get ready. Because if you acknowledge his birth, if you are on your guard, if you lay a stake in his claim that God can burst through and change the world, then he'll have no choice but to begin that change in you. Remember who we're waiting for.

Guide our waiting

What do we long for, God?
So many things –
love, life,
but also more money, more friends, more credit, more acclaim …
We do – it may not be politically correct to admit it
or be something we would ever want to say out loud –
especially within these confines –
but you know it and we know it.

Be with us, God.
In this time of waiting and watching,
wrestle in us –
stretch our searching souls
so that we see our wants more clearly.
Help us to untie the knots we get ourselves into
by desiring what cannot complete us.
Guide our longing souls back to you.

What do we long for, God?
So many things –
a magic wand or a fairy godmother:
someone else to take over for a while;
we want to wake up and for everything to be magically
better somehow.
Voilà!
We do – we know it's not probable,
we know it's not possible –
but we wish it all the same.

God be with us.
In this time of waiting and watching,
remind us of the things we already know:
that we're all in this together
and that that's a pretty good place to be;
that prayers are empty unless
we're willing to do some work after the Amen;
that beginnings and first steps are necessary
and not naive.
Your goodness surrounds us –
may we long for more sightings of that.

God who comes to us in a baby's cry,
in a lover's touch,
in the voice of a friend,
sometimes in a desperate face,
enter our yearning spirit and,
in our waiting,
guide our longing.
Amen

Waiting is part of everything

Every *second* we exist is a gift.
Gone in a whisper,
it will not come again …
So, God of us all,
we come to you and ask that you help us unwrap it,
and teach us to share it,
and call us to cherish it –
this precious life we've been given.

And there are gifts we can offer each other:
time, forgiveness, consideration …
things we cannot purchase,
but which are priceless.
And there are lessons we desperately need to learn –
about love that does what it says,
about concern that changes our behaviour,
about this life we've been given that
explodes in beauty
when we understand how to give it up.

During this time of Advent waiting,
help us to realise that there are things that need doing now.
Waiting is part of everything,
but there are times when we are guilty of being stagnant.

When we withhold forgiveness,
forgive us.
When we withhold help or mercy or a kind word,

forgive us.
When we relax in our comfort zones
even though it causes others pain,
move us.

God upon whom we wait,
wake us up.

During this time of Advent,
help us to wait and watch and expect the unexpected:
that the poor will be filled with good things,
that the oppressed will receive justice,
that you, God,
and we,
will intervene.
We dare to expect that,
because we wait on you, Lord,
and waiting is part of everything.

'Are you the one who is to come?'

'Are you the one who is to come,
or are we to wait for another?'
And then we are asked the question:
'What do you hear and see?' …

Loving God, we see
our lover's smile,
our children laughing,
our tables full and our friends
sitting around them.
When we open our eyes,
we see beauty at every turn –
and are amazed that we passed it by so often.
So thank you,
for all the blessings rained upon us.

'Are you the one who is to come,
or are we to wait for another?'
And then we are asked the question:
'What do you hear and see?' …

Loving God, we see a world that waits –
for justice to be done,
for love to conquer all,
for someone to do something for the lovers who fear
and the children who cry,
for someone to fill the empty tables and the flagging,
exhausted souls

of the ones who cannot see beauty
through their despair.
And we might shut them out, God.
Drown their calls by cranking up our Christmas carols –
but your Advent challenge is persistent
and the words have been turned on us:

'Are you the one who is to come,
or are we to wait for another?'
And because we wait for you,
we ask you today:
'Make us more like you.'
Help us to bring glad tidings,
to heal the broken-hearted,
to proclaim liberty to the captives
and release to the prisoners.
Guide our Advent waiting
and our Christmas wanting.

What in the world are we waiting for, God?

What in the world are we waiting for, God?
Well, I guess it depends on where you sit.
In some places we wait for the sales to start
and parties to crank up.
We wait for noise and music and laughter …
We wait for food and fun to fill us with cheer.
You are the life of the party.

God of all, help us to be careful and considered.
Help us to fill our lives with good things.
In a world where there is so much stuff to be had,
help us to wait for what is real.
In a world where success is measured in money and possessions,
help us not to fall into the trap
of trying to satisfy our souls with things,
which do not satisfy an eternal yearning.
Jesus Christ, help us to wait for you.

What in the world are they waiting for, God?
Well, I guess it depends on where you sit.
In some places they wait for life to start,
and life to end:
existence a reality that cannot be covered up or
filled with fluff.
The easy life with extras, a party
they weren't invited to.

God upon whom we wait,
we bring our world to you
and ask for your help,
not that you will wave a magic wand
and all will be fed,
but so that you open our hearts to the reality of our privilege –
that we realise the power of caring enough to share.

What in the world are we waiting for, God?
Good question.
Call us to look for the answers together.

What do people wait for?

What do people wait for?
Some wait to be noticed.
Others wait for folk to forget.

They wait to be born.
They wait to die.
They wait for the bus.
Seems like we are always waiting …

But during Advent, we don't just wait – we expect:
that the poor will be filled with good things,
that the oppressed will receive justice,
that God will intervene.
We dare to expect that,
because we wait on the Lord –
and waiting and expectation journey side by side
into Advent.

Jesus Christ, Truth-we-seek,
guide our waiting and watching and wondering hearts.
Shine in our lives like the beacon that brought
the wise ones to your side,
and when we find you,
may the angel-messengers call us to lay down our gifts.

What do people wait for?
Some wait to be noticed.
Others wait for folk to forget.

They wait to be born.
They wait to die.
They wait for the bus.
Seems they're always waiting …

Maybe they're waiting for us?
Maybe they're waiting for us
to notice their need and respond.
Maybe they're waiting for us to forgive
and forget the things they did that hurt us.
Maybe those who will be born into the world we leave them
are waiting for us to realise they are coming
so that we make room.
And maybe the ones who are dying
simply want someone to hold their hand.

Jesus Christ, Truth-we-seek,
as waiting and expectation board the bus into Advent,
keep them looking for the others who wait.

Waiting in taxing times

God of our waiting, in these days,
a decree goes out to all the world,
for these are taxing times …
and we are called again to go to Bethlehem,
no matter the state of our health or our world,
for we have heard the message,
we have dreamed the dream
that you will come among us …
so thank you –
for your hinting and expecting and encouraging Spirit
that has always been with you and with us.

God of our waiting, these are taxing times …
some folk journey looking for a sign,
others huddle on hillsides,
while others,
resplendent in cold palaces,
nervously wait for news that the jig is up,
and they're out.
Because the heavens have been whispering
that you are to be born
among us/one of us/one with us …
and if we allow your birth,
then things will change …

God of our waiting,
help us make straight our paths;
help us find the ones that lead to justice and peace and

love and equality ...
the ones that lead to you.

As we listen for the Word made flesh coming among us,
as we strain our ears
for the voices heralding a king
and singing to a baby,
help us not to block out those voices crying in the wilderness
they find themselves in ...

(Concerns of the day ...)

We pray for your hurting ones,
your frightened ones,
your sick and dying ones ...
Help us to comfort them.
Help us to remember that the Word is made flesh in us ...
Amen

ON THE INFANT

Bible readings

Psalm 103
Psalm 139:1–18
Luke 2:1–40
Luke 18:15–17
John 1:14

A prayer for Elin

Elin, what can we say? – welcome home. It's been a long miraculous journey for you; in the quiet darkness of the womb, all alone you waited. Warm and sheltered, hidden in your harbour, you couldn't have known: safely cosseted by the song of your mother's heartbeat, your father's muffled assurances, the family's expectant hopes for your safe arrival. And arrive you did – with all the fanfare of any birth. Into arms that held you, eyes that scanned your every feature, willing them into their memories, into a whole community of people who had already fallen in love with you sight unseen. And there will be more to come, Elin – best friends, first loves, rites of passage, new beginnings – a few closed doors, but with every one, we pray for an open window. There will be brand-new things to discover: we pray that you will embrace them. There will be disappointments and hurts: we pray for people there to help you and hold you. With every step you take on this long, miraculous journey, we pray for the company of Christ in the people who walk with you. Elin, what can we say? We say welcome.

God in the face of an infant (a mother's thought)

Incarnation: suddenly it's there and I understand its power. As you stretch slowly, arms above your head in your newly found freedom, I realise with visceral familiarity – *I've met that elbow somewhere before* … In the womb, even then you made your first bids for freedom, pushing against my body, and now you rest in my arms; yet, still you stretch. Keep on – for that is what you are called to do … Stretch towards others, reach for new insights, lean towards God like a young plant instinctively turns towards the sun. I see a spark of the Divine in your newborn face. Fresh from forever … Thank you, God. Incarnation.

'I know you …' (Psalm 139:1–18)

When Alex, our firstborn, came into the world, there was a jumble of feelings. Here was this tiny new stranger we had created together. A little person who was going to change everything! We were responsible. I mean, she was up to us …

Before her birth I had imagined every part of her, but when she arrived – I was *overwhelmed* by her completeness. And hours new and she had a mind all her own. Right from the start, she wouldn't settle on her back or on her side – the positions all the leaflets told us were correct. As long as we held her, she was fine, but the minute we tried to put her down that way, she woke up and howled …

After a rather sleepless few nights in the hospital, the Sister suggested we go ahead and try her on her stomach. Alex obviously hadn't read the leaflets – she settled down almost the instant we put her in her cot, and that was her …

After the Sister left, I stared down at that tiny person. She was lying in absolute peace, with her right hand above her head, elbow out … and suddenly it registered … *'I know you. You're the wee person who's been elbowing me in the ribs all these months … You're the one who dances to the theme tune from* Neighbours, *and you're the one who took serious personal offence to that chicken tikka.'* And then I knew even more than I had a moment before: she was mine and I was hers: we belonged, intimately and entirely, to each other …

Holy child, born of a singing mother (Luke 1:46–55)

Holy child,
born of a singing mother,
you come into the world and call us to sing –
of the marvellous works that are to come –
of the love in our hearts when we open them to each other –
of the life that you have come to pour into us …

But so often we do not sing.
We don't even hum.
Sometimes we can't even hear the tune.

Forgive us our monotone lives,
for seeing darkness rather than light,
for hearing bad news
rather than magnificent music,
for living with dread
rather than delight.
Redeem us, enliven us …
Give us hope in our lives and a song on our lips.

Help us to sing:
help us to find our own tune in you.

Baby Jesus

What part will we play in this baby's life? When he comes, will we hold him, herald him, love him, live for him? Or will we coo at his cradle, ooh and ahh at the star, have a listen when the angels sing – and then head back to reality and wistfully wish Christmas could be all year long?

Love born to us,
live in us for life,
not just for Christmas.
Child in the manger,
grow up and take your place.

What part will we play in each other's lives? When we meet, will we hold, herald, love, live for each other? Or will we say the politically correct things, be politely sympathetic, listen and offer lip-service appropriately – then go back to the real world and wistfully wish we could be more involved with each other?

Love born to us,
live in us for life,
not just for Christmas.
Child in the manger,
grow up and take your place.

What part will this life play in our lives? … Keep us by his cradle, listening at his feet, working by his side, weeping at the foot of his cross, rejoicing at his love-story that refuses to die, even when hate and evil does its worst.

What part will we play in this baby's life? That is the question that Advent asks.

What child is this?

Look at the child you seek …

The one who is coming was heralded by the old, eccentric prophets, by a wild preacher in the desert, by hired hands dozing on a hillside and foreigners following a star …

The one who is coming was born to a child mother, birthed in a barn and sung to sleep in a cow's feeding trough …

The one who is coming grew up to teach Truth and change hearts and lift the broken …

The one who is coming is the one whose sandal John says he's not worthy to untie – the same man who, much later in our story, bends down and washes the feet of the one who will betray him, the one who will doubt him, and the one who will deny he ever even knew him … The ones who aren't worthy to untie his sandals – yet he washes their feet? Some say only God could do that.

The one who is coming is the one who desperately wants us to know him … So look up to heaven and into your hearts, for he is coming among us … he stands among us now.

Swaddling bands (a play for an all-age service)

Reading: Luke 2:12

(The actors come from behind the pulpit, chatting …)

Betty: Won't be long now, I shouldn't think. We'll need to crack on if these are going to be finished in time.

Agnes: Well, why don't we sit out here in the sun and work on them for a while – no need to be inside while it's so nice.

Betty: What a good idea! And if we're here out of the way, we won't have to listen to anybody who might have something unkind to say.

Agnes: You mean Ruth and Rachel and the gossip gang?

Betty: I'm not naming names. *(Aside whisper: 'Yes.')*

Agnes: So, when's the baby due?

Betty: Soon, by the look of her. Mary's such a young thing and so petite. She already looks like she's carrying around a melon.

Agnes: I wonder if it'll be a boy or a girl. Her cousin Elizabeth had a wee boy – if Mary had a boy, maybe they could play together.

Betty: Aye, maybe, but they live a wee ways away for them to be really pally.

Agnes: I see what you mean – but there are lots of children around here for the baby to grow up with. No way he'll be lonely. *(Notices the children)* Hello, boys and girls, how are you? I hope you don't mind if we sit here quietly and work on these swaddling bands? … Oh, thank you.

Betty: They look a bit confused, Agnes. Do you know what these are, children? Well, these are for wrapping a baby in when it's first born. We're making them for a young couple called Mary and Joseph – it's their first baby. These bands should have been wrapped round their hands during their wedding, before they were wrapped round a baby, but young folk these days – putting the cart before the horse; the wedding was a bit short-notice, but never you mind, we'll make a beautiful job for the baby. Do any of you have wee brothers or sisters? … Well, then you know how special babies are!

Agnes: Of course they do, Betty. They've been babies themselves! See *(shows a swaddling band to the children),* these are going to be gifts to say 'We're glad you're here' to the baby. Mary will wrap that wee baby up in these, and they'll keep him –

Betty: *(interjects)* Or her.

Agnes: … Warm and toastie and all snugly too. Yes, a lot of times, the bands are the same ones that the mum and dad used on their wedding day. The priest wraps their hands together and says a prayer. And sometimes, they're used when someone dies: kind of like saying goodbye and wishing someone well on their journey. It's a way for the whole community to have a part in important times in life.

Betty: Have a look at this one. We're embroidering sayings, blessings we call them, onto them as a way of saying welcome! See? *(points to words on the swaddling band)*. It means welcome. I can't wait for this baby to join our village! I just have a feeling that she or he is going to be really special.

Agnes: All babies are special, Betty. *(To the children)* When the baby's born, will you make it feel welcome? Love it, take care of it, listen to it?

Betty: We're kind of counting on you because we're getting a wee bitty old for playing games and running round. We'll just make these swaddling bands and give our love.

Agnes: Maybe you could help make some swaddling bands too? Or maybe you could think of other ways to make the baby feel welcome … What would those be? …

A prayer for parents

As a father (parent) shows compassion to his/her children, so the Lord shows compassion … (Psalm 103:13).

All parents are slightly insane: they gaze on a bald, wrinkly mix looking somewhere between Buddha and Winston Churchill – and see utter perfection. They embrace the endurance test of sleepless nights with a cranky, colicky infant – and then lie awake all night again, pretending not to wait up for a teenager researching independence. They inevitably give up a huge chunk of themselves and what they want for what their children need.

True, mothers and fathers can be a bit on the nutty side, but we get it from you, God, because when we get it right, our love mirrors yours: selfless and unconditional and endlessly smitten.

Parent of all,
forgive us when we don't make the stretch to everybody:
when we love only the ones we decide are ours,
when we ignore the cries of those who are different or distant,
when we cannot see that the family you have birthed,
the family of which we are a part,
is as vast as the ocean,
and one.

Forgive us when our love is selfish and limited.
And forgive us especially
when we teach and pass on that same selfishness to our children.
God of love, in your love,
forgive and change us.
Amen

ON MARY AND JOSEPH

Bible readings

Psalm 103:13
Proverbs 20:7
Isaiah 66:13
Matthew 1:18–25
Matthew 23:9
Luke 1–2:40
Luke 13:34
John 19:25–27
Acts 1:14

The eternal things

We travel closer to Bethlehem, and there are whispers on the wind. Mary sings: *'My soul magnifies the Lord, and my spirit rejoices in God my Saviour.'*

What do our souls magnify?
In what do our spirits rejoice?

God who calls us to Christmas,
may it be the eternal things,
and not the shiny empty ones.
As we make our way through Advent,
may we magnify love, hope, joy, peace, forgiveness –
they can be made bigger through our little efforts.

May our spirits rejoice in the unnoticed kindness,
the unexpected generosity,
the unwarranted grace.
When we are tempted to chase the baubles and tinsel
and the pretty packages;
when we become afraid and anxious,
and in some mad rush of consumerism
forget why we celebrate,
may we hear the angel echoes:
'Do not be afraid – there are tidings of great joy.'
And then may we remember.

We travel closer to Bethlehem,
and there are whispers on the wind.

Don't you hear Mary singing?
What do our souls magnify?
In what do our spirits rejoice?

God of love,
may they be the eternal things.
Amen

Promise to Mary

'Do not be afraid …
For nothing will be impossible with God.'
God, forgive us when that scares the life out of us –
when that belief –
when we let it penetrate our souls –
is enough to send us scurrying back to the familiar,
hiding our hearts in our hands
and holding back the things
we have learned to believe
will keep us safe.

Christ who walks beside us,
forgive us when the last thing we want
is for 'the power of the Most High'
to overshadow us.
Forgive us when we prefer to lurk inside more comfortable,
less frightening and challenging
shadows.

This is the God who scatters the proud,
and we can be prideful;
this is the God who brings down the powerful,
and we value power;
this is the God who sends the rich away empty,
and we cling to the belief that things will satisfy us.

Christ who wants to be born in us,
stretch our stingy souls

so that we might magnify you in our lives.
Help us to be strong enough to be weak and vulnerable;
fill us with good things
so that we can lay down selfish satisfactions
that ultimately leave us
empty.

In your mercy,
help your servants here to not be afraid,
for nothing will be impossible with you, God.

What have we done to Mary?

What have we done to Mary? Dressed her in blue, put an ethereal smile on her face and placed her heavily pregnant frame somehow delicately upon a donkey.

What have we done to Mary? Made her an eternal virgin and a saintly mother – sweetness and light and maternal wisdom all rolled up into one perfect, unattainable ideal.

What have we done to Mary? Captured her within the verses of 'Silent night', 'Away in a manger', 'Love came down at Christmas' – all calm and bright with a baby who never cries, and love keeping everybody nice and warm and tucked up …

My, how we have tried to tame Mary, but what a story she has to tell – and she will not be silenced. Etched into this epic story of the birth of goodness – Godness – Mary's song reminds us of eternal truths, if we will allow her to escape and find voice. Please understand, this story is beautiful and I have no desire to tear it apart or untell the magic and mystery, but it has so much more to offer, if we'll just free Mary and let her really sing.

She sings a song to Elizabeth that heralds a new day – they are an unlikely pairing and that is part of the setting of this story: the two improbable women whose conditions clearly shout that nothing is impossible with God and that God will very often surprise us. An old barren woman heavy with child, and a virgin girl, inexplicably pregnant, warn us that what's to come will break through the barriers of what we think we know. You don't find imagery more powerful than that. And what about the message of justice and peace in her melody – of the world turned upside down? It is not an introduction to her son echoed in our lullabies.

Just a girl

She wasn't a woman – she was a girl, just a child herself. I don't think we *really* realise that – her pedestal has been built up so high it's hard for us to see her any more. And it must have been so scary – what would her parents say? What would her husband-to-be say? She only had the word of an angel – if that's what that was … maybe it was a dream, a vision, a desperate wish from a terrified girl. Upside down and inside out … that's what happened to her life – with this tiny, fragile, unexpected life growing inside her. She was expecting!

And she wasn't a woman – she was only a girl. And she didn't do anything special. Well, that's not true. She didn't do anything special – except say 'Yes'. She said 'Yes' to God, and because she did, nothing was ever to be the same – anywhere. She brought a child into the world … She brought the Light of the world into the world … But how could she know? I mean, really know. She was just a girl.

I gave him a name (Luke 2:21)

I gave him a name – he needed a name. We all need to know who we are. I gave him the name Jesus: the name the angel whispered in my ear. And I gave him a family – everybody needs a family, folk who love you because you're theirs. Not much is said of that and that's fine with me – I didn't do it to gain recognition or status. I don't really know why I did it. At the time, things were so unreal – but the baby was definitely real and so was the danger to its mother if I didn't do the right thing. I just needed to figure out what that was. I decided at some point that the right thing was love. The right thing was trust. The right thing was the hardest road, and so we started down it together.

I gave him a name – he needed a name. We all need to know who we are. And I don't think we really understood who he was or that that name would echo through time – long after our journey was through. I gave him the name Jesus: the name the angel whispered in my ear – and now it whispers in your hearts as you sit here in the quiet of this night.

I gave him a family – everybody needs a family, folk who love you because you're theirs. And I don't think we really understood who he would add to our family – who he'd gather to himself: how he'd make you all not just his family, but his body, his very soul.

It was the right thing – love. The right thing often leads you onto the hardest road, but it's also the most beautiful. Let's start down it together.

ON THE STAR

Bible readings

Genesis 1:1–5;14–19
Job 38:4–7
Psalm 8
Psalm 19:1
Matthew 2:1–12
Mark 13:24–25
Revelation 22:16

A beautiful clear night

From deep within my childhood memories, I see clear starlit nights. They came mostly in the autumn, when the air was beginning to get that hint of winter and even the colours seemed more alive, the earth expectant. I loved that sense of something coming.

We lived on a lake, so I would sometimes go down to the dock at the bottom of our property and stretch myself out and just look up. The water would move beneath and the boards would creak and the waves would rock you like a song – and all around was just deep dark blue and open space and stars.

Close your eyes and imagine it for a moment: a beautiful clear night – lying on your back, stretched out all alone, surrounded by water and waves, staring up at a blue sea of stars …

That's when I figured out that there had to be something more (God): something hovering just beyond the tangible … I still can't put it into words – for all my love of what can be spoken, *that* cannot be expressed any other way than in the speechless peace that overwhelms your soul as it rocks in a sea of stars.

How far away's a star?

How far away's a star?
Light filtering through the aeons;
floating through time, setting the nothingness alight –
chink in the vast inky black.
5.88 million million miles equals one light year …
A miraculous distance to travel
to soften the night for a baby.
Bathed in the light of a million million miles' journey,
he turns towards the light of a star
and the warmth of a woman
and the welcome of a world
sore in need of light.

ON THE WISE MEN

Bible readings

Proverbs 8:1–11
Proverbs 9:1–10
Matthew 2:1–12
John 1:1–5; 10 –14
1 Corinthians 1:25
Colossians 2:2–3

The wise started early

In the tale the sages tell, the wise started early – the moment there was a gleam in their deep-blue sky, they set out. They'd been waiting, you see – waiting and watching, and they knew that hope was near. They'd planned, packed what they needed, and laid the rest aside. For their journey, they would need light hearts, clear minds, patient feet.

In the tale the sages tell, the wise started early – the moment there was a gleam in their deep-blue sky, they set out.

And now we follow their footsteps – the ones long time ago left in the sand. Wait and watch, for hope is near … consider what you carry with you and carefully lay aside what you do not need. Unpack the dreams of your heart and carry them like a gift to lay at his infant feet when you find him. Advent is close, expectation is holding its breath. The angels hover high above. Come, begin your journey.

Time will tell

We don't know how many there were, but there were three gifts: so we decided that there were three. And they set off just about the same time the angel whispered to Mary that she was pregnant, a wee bit before Joseph found out he was going to be a father. Who am I talking about? That's right – the wise men. Have you ever wondered why they were wise? Well, I can tell you why. They were wise because they believed in goodness. They believed that being kind was more important than being powerful. They believed that love was the strongest force on earth, and they were patient. They were willing to wait for love. Whenever people asked them how they knew that love was strongest, they always said: *'Time will tell.'*

One day, they saw a star shining really brightly in the sky and they decided they should follow it. They had read that a star might be a sign that an important baby was going to be born. So they set off. As they walked through the desert and watered their camels and kept up with the star, they said to each other: *'Time will tell.'*

They followed the star all the way to Jerusalem. Now Jerusalem was a place where an important person lived – Herod, who was a king of the Jews. Now Herod wasn't very wise. He believed exactly the opposite of what the wise men believed. He believed that being powerful was more important than being kind. He believed that being in control was the most important thing on earth, and he was nervous. He was always afraid that somebody stronger would come and take away all the things he'd taken. You see, Herod stole from poorer, weaker people. Whenever he was challenged or questioned he said: *'Might makes right.'*

The wise men got to Jerusalem, and decided to ask Herod if he knew anything about the star. They didn't know he was such a greedy, nervous king or they wouldn't have bothered. Herod got scared when he heard that they were looking for a baby king. He thought this new king might want all his stuff. So he tried to trick the wise men. He told them that if they found this baby, they were to come back and tell him so he could go and worship him. They saw right through that. They got back on their camels and followed the star to Bethlehem. And guess what they found? They found out that kindness was more important than being powerful, that love was the strongest force on earth. They met the baby King and knew that they would go home changed forever. That is their story. For the rest of their lives, whenever people asked them how they knew that love ruled over everything, they always said: *'Time will tell.'*

Whenever you do something kind, you are telling time that love rules. Whenever you listen, care, forgive, share, hold somebody's hand when they're sad, you are saying to time that love is in charge. Learn a lesson from the wise men.

ON SHEPHERDS

Bible readings

Psalm 22
Psalm 23
Ezekiel 34
Matthew 5:1–12
Luke 2:8–20
John 10

Sounds so romantic

'In that region, there were shepherds living in the fields, keeping watch over their flocks by night.' (Luke 2:8)

Sounds so romantic – Christmas-cake perfection with a little icing sugar sprinkled over like fairy dust.

When actually …

In that region, lived the poorest of the poor, holed up, huddled together on a hill putting their lives at risk to protect someone else's livelihood.

In that region, the margin between rich and poor people gaped vast and ugly – and the angels had the audacity to sing about good news to the likes of them! And they had the audacity to listen …

And what about today? If the angels spread their golden wings and swooped down from on high, where would this heavenly host appear – singing of glory and saying: *'Do not be afraid'*?

Well perhaps …

In that region, where homeless live in shelters and under bridges and on friend's settees for a time and in bedsits when the government gets its act together …

In that region, where children are afraid to go outside; children who've learned that they can't expect much from the world they've been dropped into and that's promptly let them fall through the cracks.

The Christmas angels came singing *'Do not be afraid'* in fearful places. They flew first to the ones most in need of good news, least likely to be looking for it, or even expecting it, and quite frankly with more reason than most to refuse the invitation to believe in anything as unlikely as hope.

It is said that angels are simply God's messengers – bringing with them a simple, if unbelievable, possibility: 'It doesn't have to be this way,' they say. 'Come and see this new thing that has been made known.'

If there is to be a stirring of angel wings, a new song building in the air, then in this region God's messengers (you and me minus the haloes) have to be audacious enough to sing in fearful places.

Seems shepherds always get the worst of it …

Seems shepherds always get the worst of it …
Cold hillsides and rocky, barren places …
Sheep and sheep and more sheep – and sleepless nights counting them.
No camels to ride or gifts to bear, no wisdom either – just second-hand news.

Seems shepherds always get the worst of it …
Bathrobes and tea towels and the back of the stage – sharing one line:
'Let us go to Bethlehem and see this thing that has been made known to us.'
No tinsel or glitter or golden wings.

Seems shepherds always get the worst of it …
Minimum wage and zero-hours contracts.
No pension plan or savings account – no respect either.
Just systemic injustice that keeps them in their lowly places.

Seems they had something in common with the baby they visited.
Later, he would call himself a shepherd.
Later, he would lay aside his wants for the needs of his sheep.
Later, he would say 'If you love me, you will feed my lambs.'
In the face of the worst, he would give his best.
So there is wisdom.
There is glory without the gold.
And there is hope that there will be justice for those who always
seem to get the worst of it.

ON ANGELS

Bible readings

Psalm 103:19–22
Mark 1:13
Luke 1:26–38
Luke 2:8–14
John 20:12
Hebrews 13:2

What sweeter music? (an address to Dunblane High School students)*

What sweeter music can we bring than angel song?

Well, what about forgiveness – that's pretty sweet – especially if you're the one waiting for the forgiveness. Is there somebody you need to forgive, something you're clinging to – refusing to let go.

What sweeter music can we bring? Well, what about peace – that's pretty sweet – ask the ones living in war-torn places around the globe. Ask the ones who fear the outside, who fear the darkness, or crave it …

What sweeter music can we bring? How about time, love, friendship? You fill in the blanks …

There's a reason we celebrate his birth in the dark of December – and it's not because it was his birthday: we don't really know when that was. No, it's deeper than that – more visceral … It's in the dark that we really appreciate, crave the light. It's when things are most desperate that kindness, mercy, justice and peace shine like beacons showing people what home might look like.

What sweeter music can we bring?

Last night there was a carol service at Cornton Vale prison, and there will be one like it at Polmont Young Offenders Institute later this week. Both are practically on our doorstep, but they're a world away. 5th- and 6th-year students, did you know that there are prisoners in those institutions who are younger than you are? What did they do to get themselves there? Lots of things … Do they deserve to be where they are? I'll tell you what they didn't deserve. They didn't deserve to be born into poverty, and statistically speaking, almost all of them were – deprivation that put them at least ten steps back from the starting line when they were still in their prams. And they didn't deserve to be introduced to drugs and alcohol before they were in their teens – and statistically speaking, almost all of them were. What sweeter music can we bring?

Well, maybe a bit of justice for folk before the long arm of the law has no choice but to intervene.

At St Blane's Church this afternoon, the local Boy's Brigade will be waiting for Dunblane to respond to a plea from the food bank in Alloa – they've been inundated with requests for food, clothing, toys. Times are hard and when you get paid minimum wage, or less if you're a young person, and life wasn't stable before something went wrong, you can be left in crisis. It happens. What sweeter music can we bring? Maybe a little help for people who need it. The Boy's Brigade will be there from 4:00 to 6:00 tonight.

What sweeter music can we bring than a carol to sing to celebrate the birth of this, our heavenly King?

Well, what about forgiveness, peace, justice, love? How about time, friendship, empathy? You fill in the blanks … The man this baby grew up to be spoke a challenge to those who would follow him. He said that you would find him in the eyes of the poor, the prisoner, the stranger – he said that God lived in them. So, what sweeter music can we bring? I think the sweetest sound that comes to God's ears is the sound of change. Happy Christmas, Dunblane High School.

* A reflection on 'A Christmas Carol, Sung to the King in the Presence at White-Hall', by Robert Herrick (1591-1674)

Personal note

'Peace on earth, goodwill to all' – that's the message the angels sang. But I thought I'd get a bit more personal.

So, to you with wee ones around you this year, I wish you the joy that only comes from seeing Christmas through your children's eyes. I wish you patience and a sense of humour at one o'clock Christmas morning when the 'easy to assemble' gift from Santa is still lying in pieces on the living room floor – and I wish you a long nap on Boxing Day.

To you of the empty nest, I wish you a sense of adventure on this new part of the journey – and a wicked self-satisfaction when you look at the knackered faces of your younger counterparts!

If this has been a hard year, if the hype and good cheer rings hollow, I hope and pray you don't suffer the sadness alone, but that love wings its way to you, that we out here find ways to find each other.

'Peace on earth, goodwill to all' – that's the message the angels sang. Let's all get a bit more personal than that this year, and start where we are.

How to refuse an angel: most highly favoured lady 1

'You are *just* the person I wanted to see.' He said it with such charm and innocence – he was obviously a pro. 'When this position opened, I immediately thought of you. You would love it – the hours are flexible and you can come and go as you please. You can even take the children with you if you need to. I don't think it would be a problem, once they got used to it.'

She immediately started with her counter moves. 'I've flexed my time about as much as it can be flexed. I'm already working at the hospital part-time and the girls are awfully wee. My husband's already working two jobs, so he can't really help out any more, and I don't want to leave the kids if I can help it.'

She thought that body blow would end it, but he'd only just begun. He sighed in that unnervingly understanding way. 'It's just that we need a feminine touch. There are a lot of wards with women who are kind of afraid of men and we need a balance. You've done this kind of work before – just think about it. Pray about it and I'll get back to you.'

He must have sensed weakness because he went on: 'I'll even go with you and give you a tour of the place. Then you can say yes!'

And there she was – stitched up, or so she felt. So, she went with him and she saw what he meant and she flexed a bit further …

And she was the one who was blessed. Her time working at the residential facility for folk with severe learning disabilities was hard, and took a lot of growing on her part, but it taught her things she never would have, could have learned anywhere else. She met James – who could play football without a ball and commentate on his imaginary game with such perfection that you thought there was a radio playing. He taught her that joy is a pure thing. It doesn't need to be questioned all the time and you don't have to have anything to have it.

She met Sadie – who was time-consuming and annoying and attention-seeking in the extreme. But she taught her that there are some people who just need you, and you just have to be there. They don't play by your rules and they never will. But that doesn't make them less important.

She met Sam and his carers, and that's what they were – carers. Sam had autism and he spent his day spinning around the common room. Most of the time he was quite happy, but sometimes he'd get to spinning too fast one way and start to get agitated. When his carers saw this happening, one of them would yell: 'Sam, son – turn yourself around and spin the other way!' And he would and he'd be fine. From Sam and his carers she learned probably the most profound lesson: sometimes, when you're getting agitated, you just need to turn the other way, and sometimes it's your friends who tell you to turn.

There are so many more people and lessons and memories that have held her in good stead … And to think, she thought she'd been stitched up. Being a blessing blesses you. Strange how that works out.

How to refuse an angel: most highly favoured lady 2

And he came to her, and he said: 'Greetings, favoured one! The Lord is with you.' But she was much perplexed by his words and pondered what sort of greeting this might be. Smart girl – to have pondered the greeting. But he'd said it with such charm and innocence – he was obviously a pro. And he told her a wondrous story of what might be. She was chosen, perfect for the job. 'She would conceive and carry a son …'

She immediately started with her counter moves. 'How can this be? I'm only a girl and I don't know anything about men yet … I can't be a mother – I'm still a child.'

She thought that body blow would end it, but he'd only just begun. He sighed in that unnervingly understanding way. 'Mary, the Holy Spirit will come upon you and the power of the Most High will overshadow you; therefore, the child to be born will be holy: he will be called Son of God.'

He must have sensed weakness because he went on: 'Nothing will be impossible with God.' And there she was – stitched up, or so she felt.

So, she went along with him and she saw the possibilities of what he meant and she said 'Yes'. She was a blessing, and she was blessed. Strange how that works out.

The choice she made that day brought hard times, times when she had to really trust and grow, but He (her child) taught her things she never would have, could have learned anywhere else. He taught her about love – love that doesn't depend on what you do or don't do, but just loves. He taught her about power – real power that comes from being brave enough to allow yourself to be completely vulnerable. He taught her about forgiveness – not a token trivial 'don't worry about it' – forgiveness that doesn't pass the surface – but a 'Father, forgive them for they don't know what they're doing' kind of forgiveness that resurrects dead lives. And because of her 'Yes', He taught us too – and the whole world is resurrected through Him. All because she believed that nothing is impossible with God.

So, what will you do next time it happens, because it will, you know? … What will you do when you get tapped on the shoulder and someone says: 'Greetings, favoured one! The Lord is with you'?

After you've pondered what sort of greeting this might be, what will you do? Will you plan your counter moves and dodge the question? Will you come up with a really good, incredibly legitimate reason for telling them they've got the wrong person … or will you believe that nothing is impossible with God, and say 'Yes'? Being a blessing somehow blesses you. Strange how that works out.

Ready-made angel: a Christmas Eve play

As the minister speaks, the angel (dressed in wings and an apron and carrying a duster) begins to make his/her way down the central aisle, dusting, cleaning ...

Minister: *(to congregation)* It's almost time, you know. Are you ready? Well, we here at the Cathedral *(church ...)* definitely are. The Advent candles are lit, the tree is up, the Christingle bags are out, and in a minute we'll all be putting them together. I've delivered my Christmas cards and – *(notices the angel and stops speaking)* ...

Angel: *(The angel notices that the talking has stopped and looks up.)* Sorry, I didn't mean to disturb you – just checking that everything's ready.

Minister: I can assure you – everything's ready for Christmas. Who are you anyway?

Angel: *(points to wings)* I thought that was kind of obvious: I'm an angel.

Minister: But what are you doing here? It's Christmas Eve – shouldn't you be away somewhere singing or delivering a message – you know, angel stuff?

Angel: Well, I *am* delivering a message. The message is YOU'RE NOT AS READY AS YOU THINK YOU ARE.

Minister: What are you talking about? Look at the tree, the Advent candles – all these people. We're ready.

Angel: What about the baby?

Minister: What do you mean, the baby?

Angel: The baby that's going to be born tonight.

Minister: But he's not really being born … it's just a celebration.

Angel: If you say so … But, I am the angel *(turns to go).*

Minister: W … Wait a minute. Not that I believe you, but just supposing … what would we need, for a baby?

Angel: A baby needs to be warm. The most important thing a new baby needs – anybody needs – is to know they're wanted and welcome.

Minister: A blanket would keep the baby warm and make him, or her, feel secure.

Angel: Good idea. Arms are good too. Sometimes hugs can be as good as a blanket. Remember that.

Minister: Ahh … OK, anyway, I don't think we have anything like that around here.

Angel: Are you sure? Maybe some of these children would look under the pews. There might be something unexpected. It is Christmas Eve. Go on – have a look … Any luck? If you've found a blanket, bring it up and place it in the manger. *(A child brings the blanket up.)*

Minister: I can't imagine where that came from.

Angel: Welcomes come from the most unexpected places – especially on Christmas Eve.

Minister: What else do we need, just in case?

Angel: Another thing that babies want – everybody wants – is a little light in dark places. It's comforting and makes them feel safe.

Minister: We don't have that either. We've got the Cathedral lights, but those go out when we leave.

Angel: I think I saw a lantern at the back of the Cathedral – in one of the pews. Could the person sitting next to it bring it up here, or give it to someone nearby to bring it? … *(The light is brought forward.)* There. That's better.

Minister: Well, I have to admit – it *is* looking a lot cosier up here now. I suppose the only thing left is food. The baby will need something to eat.

Angel: His mum can sort that out, but she and the dad will probably be starving. What about something for them?

Minister: I don't think there's any food in the Cathedral.

Angel: You keep forgetting that it's Christmas Eve and unexpected things happen tonight. I think there might be something in the pulpit.

Minister: Does someone want to go up and see? *(A bag of food, goodies is brought forward.)* OK, I think we're ready now – ready for Jesus to be born.

Angel: Who said I was talking about Jesus?

Minister: But you said –

Angel: I said, 'Are you ready for the baby that's going to be born tonight?' And there will be many babies born tonight. They all need a welcome, and warmth, a little light for their journey and a fair share of food. When Jesus was grown up he told us to always remember that he can be found in the little ones, the unlikely ones, the unexpected one – so be ready.

Minister: *(disappointedly):* So, he's not really being born … it's just a celebration?

Angel: If you say so … But, I am the angel. *(The angel turns and goes.)*

I've got a message for you

Voice 1: I've got a message for you.

Voice 2: It could be important.

Voice 3: Life-changing even.

Voice 1: Or it could be as simple as 'take out the rubbish'.

Voice 2: Remember the milk.

Voice 3: Pick up the dry cleaning.

(Pause)

Voice 1: I've got a message for you.

Voice 2: It could be important.

Voice 3: Life-changing even.

Voice 1: And it could be as simple as love …

Voice 2: Listen …

Voice 3: Learn …

Voice 1: I've got a message for you.

Voice 2: It could be important.

Voice 3: Life-changing even.

Prayer to the angels

Sung response: 'All night, all day, angels watchin' over me, my Lord …'
(Traditional)

Watch over them tonight:
the little ones and the lost ones …
the frightened ones and the forsaken ones …
the dying and the desperate ones …
for they need the hovering shelter of your wings.

Sung response

Wish over them tonight:
people's plans and potential,
people's hopes
daring to raise their heads above the parapet of uncertainty,
insights that are finding their feet and their voices.
They need the power of your prayers
if they are to become more than just a thought,
however good.

Sung response

Want for them tonight:
peace, joy, wisdom, justice, freedom, love.
Want it for everyone,
no exceptions.
Flood the skies with a lullaby
and a love song for the weary world,
for we all need angel voices pleading our case,

praying for change,
embracing the earth
with a bit of heaven.

Sung response

(Prayers of the day ...)

What are we expecting?

Why do we do this, year after year: looking heavenward, listening for angels, waiting for the birth? What are we hoping for? What are we expecting?

Chant: 'Over my head I hear music in the air', from *Love and Anger: Songs of Lively Faith and Social Justice,* John L. Bell and Graham Maule, Wild Goose Publications

Why do we do this, year after year: praying for peace when war surrounds, calling for calm when chaos looms, hoping for the holy in the midst of the ordinary? What is it we have heard? What are we expecting?

Chant: 'Over my head'

And so it happens – year after year – that when the world least expects it – in the dark of the night, in times of great chaos, surrounded by the lowliest and sought by the wise – that love creeps in and is born to us. The angels sing the hopeful glory of God.

Chant: 'Over my head'

ON LIGHT

Bible readings

Genesis 1:1–5
Psalm 119:105
Isaiah 9:2a
Isaiah 42:16
Matthew 5:13–16
Luke 11:33–35
John 1:3–5
John 3:18–20
Romans 13:12

This is the night

Shhh, this is the night of the story – the one that sings in our hearts, that whispers to our spirits. This is the night of the story – the one we dare to believe, even when the prudent would doubt. This is the story of the light that sparked to life that night long ago. It/He hovers here among the watchers, the listeners, the prayers … the story tells itself to those who will listen; the light shows itself to those who will see …

So gather now, open your ears and hear our story. Open the eyes of your heart, look heavenward and expect the light. Wake up your sense of wonder and worship the child who will be born for you and me and all the world … Shhh, and listen for the angel's song.

Song: 'Christ be our light' (refrain), by Bernadette Farrell, CH4

In the very beginning, there was light. It burned off the gloom of a time before creation; it warmed the earth, made things grow, gave us day and night – taught us about rest. In the very beginning, there was light …

Song: 'Christ be our light' (refrain)

In our day-to-days, there is light. It pushes through the chinks in our armour of prejudice; it finds its way into the shadows of our sorrow and fear; it floods our minds with new and grand ideas. It teaches us about change. In our day-to-days, there is light.

Song: 'Christ be our light' (refrain)

Light flashes with glimpses of the possible future – when babies laugh, children smile, people meet and walk and talk together. Minds change, love grows, what will be becomes exciting. When the future becomes full of what might be, there is light.

Song: 'Christ be our light' (refrain)

Tonight, the light of the world shines anew. It is full of possibility – born to change us, to help us find peace, to teach us to rest together.

Welcome the light that will burst through whatever darkness there is. Darkness hasn't got a chance against the love-light of God.

Come, light of God, come.
Amen

The spark (for an Advent service)

There's a story about how the world was created told in the Midrash, a collection of stories from long ago about the stories in the Bible – a way of supposing what else might have happened. We do it all the time, this supposing more. It's part of the gift God gave us in being human: we're curious and love to use our imaginations.

So imagine that when God was creating all the beautiful things we see, God also made beautiful containers to hold the divine light – a light that would radiate out like a lantern and warm everything and light up the world with God-light. But the light was so powerful that it couldn't be held and the containers shattered: divine sparks went into everything – flew deep into trees and plants and animals … The story even hints that, later on, when God created Adam and *'breathed life into his frame'*, that God was actually blowing on a divine spark and bringing it to life.

The man who told this story said that it was our job to free the sparks of God that are hidden in everything. He said that whatever we did, if we did it remembering that the sparks were there, we would free them. So if we pick up a hammer and wood and make a house for someone who is homeless, then we free the sparks. If we give a piece of bread to a hungry stranger, then we free the sparks in the grain. If we hug someone who's sad, or laugh with someone who feels joyful, we free sparks. No matter how small the act, we can free God's light and set it back into the world. What a beautiful story – I'm glad he thought it up.

Ever see a child's eyes light up – on Christmas morning when the magic and love of giving explode from them?

(Someone lights a sparkler.)

Remember the first time you looked into the eyes of the person you'd fallen in love with, and your breath caught and the wee jolt came and you both just knew?

(Someone lights a sparkler.)

Ever walked out on a snowy night into a sparkling sea of white, with the sky and the people you are with lit up with the magic of it all?

(Someone lights a sparkler.)

Ever witnessed the birth of a child? Heard the 'aha' of that first breath and then the cry? Inspected tiny perfect hands, counted toes, looked into eyes fresh from God?

(Someone lights a sparkler.)

I wonder if those were the God-sparks being set free. Tonight is about the light coming into the world – it's about the first 'aha' and then the cry. This is about the light that also couldn't be contained and sets up residence in every single person.

Song: 'O little love who comes again', by Shirley Erena Murray (tune: 'O Waly, Waly')

Funny thing about sparks, they are beautiful and they glow with such intensity, but what becomes of them?

Tonight, decide what you'll do when you see a spark: will you let it fizzle out, or will you breathe on it, protect it, fan it and let it flame into something else?

The story we end with has radiated light for over two thousand years. It has thrown its beam on justice, peace, joy. Listen to it again. Then together we will light our Christingles and celebrate. Take them home with you and put them in your window as a symbol of the light coming into the world. And as you leave, don't forget to look for the sparks.

Reading: Luke 2:1–20

Folk light their Christingles …

Longing for light

Infants and plants – all growing things – long for the light – stretch and turn towards it instinctively; yearn for what it gives unbidden: warmth and a stirring – inner strength and outer stretch! And in this most sacred of seasons, it is no different: the world still looks longingly for the light of the world; it shushes itself as it listens more closely for the Word made flesh to speak that he has again come among us …

Jesus, light of the world,
forgive us when our words or thoughts or attitudes or actions
dim your light and muffle your words
or stall your coming …

Forgive us when we don't even look for your shining any more,
but are content to sit in our half-light
and moan about the darkness …

Forgive us when we complain
that we don't understand other people any more,
yet are not content to listen to them when they try to explain …

And forgive us when we feel the stirring of your birth in us,
but push you back or away
or ignore you completely.

For all these things,
and for the things we admit in silence

and in the dark,
Lord of light,
Word made flesh,
forgive us …
Turn on the light that stirs our souls.

Shine

In a sad and sorrowful corner,
just a chink of light can abolish the darkness.

Where life is stifled and stale,
just a hint of a breeze can quicken the spirit.

The birth of a tiny baby heralds a new way
even when all hell breaks loose
and Herods reign supreme.

Light of the world,
Spirit's breath,
body of Christ,
come and shine.

Can you see the light?

Voice 1: Can you see the light? *(Someone stands up and lights a lantern.)* It hovers on the hillside, just a glimmer. Barely noticeable, but there nevertheless. Children, turn to the nearest grown-up and, on the count of three, ask: 'Can you see it?' 1, 2, 3 …

Voice 2: Can you see the light? *(Someone stands up and lights a lantern.)* It casts out the darkest shadows, and when we're afraid, it can calm and comfort us. Adults, turn to the nearest child and, on the count of three, ask: 'Can you see it?' 1, 2, 3 …

The love of God is ready to be born again – will He find home in our hearts?

It's Christmas Eve – can you see the light?

(Place a lantern in the pulpit.)

The light of the world wants to shine

Light-shine, love-never-lost … it's almost time to be born.
If the stories are true, you live in each of us
and come shining through in the most unexpected places.
Who will you be, where will you find us,
when you come and slip in beside?
Where will you bid us shine?

Song: 'Jesus bids us shine' (traditional) (verse 1)

Baby boy,
we pray that we will see you for who you are
and that we will welcome you.
When you stand in the shoes of the poor,
we pray that we do not react with contempt or condescension.
When you come as a stranger,
we pray that we are not immediately suspicious.
When you look up at us in the face of a child,
we pray that we are patient and kind,
and remember what it's like
to be new to the planet.

As we wait for your birth,
as we wonder how and who you'll be this time,
we pray that we never stop looking for you
in the light of each other.

When we fail,
forgive and turn us round;

when we wander down the wrong paths,
guide our steps back.
The light of the world wants to shine –
keep us from being dim –
bid us shine.

Song: 'Jesus bids us shine' (verse 3)

So, what lies behind darkness?

So, what lies behind darkness?
Some see the dawn – glimmers of light flecked with gold and red.

For times when we are gifted with the sight of a new beginning,
edging up through a hard-tipped lesson,
thank you, God.
For times when friends turn the light on when the room is pitch-black,
thank you, God.
For times when we realise that the beauty of yesterday outweighs
the heartache we had to endure:
that tomorrow will be a better place because of the love we knew –
thank you, God.

So, what lies behind the darkness?
Some cannot imagine – they endure endless night:
the gloom of war, sickness, poverty, and other people's apathy …

Help us, God of all,
to learn the lessons of history
that we might turn on the light.

They say you're coming in a cloud with power and great glory.
They say we'll see the signs,
like the first leaves on a tree or the feel of the sun on our backs
that heralds a change in season.
They say to be on guard, to be alert, to be ready.
Ready for what?

Christ who comes in the name of the Lord,
Messiah who proclaims that the kingdom of God is near,
prophet who dares preach good news to the poor,
help us to turn on the light,
because the dark is such a powerful foe.
It keeps us from seeing each other.

In a world where so many go hungry,
while we plan our Christmas feast,
in a world where some children have nothing
while others have so much that they are losing their ability
to imagine,
in a world where war visits time and time again,
especially fond of its poorest relations,
help us to turn on the light.
Amen

ON GIFTS

Bible readings

Matthew 2:11
Matthew 6:19–21
1 Corinthians 12:4–11
2 Corinthians 9:6–9
James 1:17–18

Presents

Presence.

Wrapped and waiting – the present.
Needed and now within reach – the present.
Yours for the giving/yours for the taking – the present.

Open the eyes of your heart,
the ears of your spirit,
the hands made for helping,
and offer your present.

Where your treasure lies (Matthew 6:21)

Once upon a time, there was a young man; one much like the ones you've known. He had barely begun his journey, and potential and promise surrounded his every step. One day, very much like today, he set out walking – to find a treasure lying by the side of the road. Looking up and down the path, he saw no one nearby, so he picked it up. It was beautiful and seductive, glistening in his hand as it caught the light. *Who could ever leave behind something of this beauty?* he wondered. *Who could put it aside – even for a minute?* Not believing his good fortune, he glanced up and down the road again, just in case someone had appeared to reclaim their treasure. Then, shaking his head in disbelief, he began to walk away, tossing the treasure into the air and catching it, whistling as he went.

Then, suddenly, as he rounded a corner, in front of him stood a gnarled old woman. 'You have taken my treasure,' she said. 'But I will let you keep it, for I've had it long enough and I've wearied of it … There is only one thing I must tell you: This treasure holds both a blessing and a curse; for although it belongs to you now and to no one else, if you ever put it down for any reason, it may be taken from you. You must hold it in your hands or risk losing it forever.'

The young man was very young indeed, and did not understand why anyone would give up such a wonderful thing, so he hastily thanked the old woman and left before she could change her mind. He glanced back once, just to make sure the old woman wasn't following him, but saw only a young girl – carefree and happy – skipping across a field.

Well, years went by, and the young man held on to his treasure. He adjusted his way of doing things so that his treasure was always with him. At first, it did not seem like too much of a chore; but as the years went by, the treasure seemed to grow larger and more cumbersome. The day came when he could no longer hold it in the palm of one hand, and needed both hands to carry it. Still, he simply could not put it down and risk losing it, so he continued on, adjusting his ways more and more to accommodate his treasure.

Without his even realising it, the treasure began to take over. He saw adventures come and go – things that would have taken his fancy had he not been afraid to take his eye off the treasure. He saw friends in need of help, but his hands were now full and there was no room for them any more. One day, he saw a child from the street stumble and fall, but could not bring himself to offer his hands. He became so preoccupied with holding on to his treasure that life and love, potential and promise – those things that had courted him in his youth – seemed to elude him. And the saddest thing of all was that he had ceased even to notice.

So many days came and went in his life. One day he met a beautiful girl who touched his heart, and she wanted to hold his hand, but he couldn't take the risk and, eventually, even she went away.

Day by day, year by year, the treasure became more awkward to carry, evermore cumbersome, until the young man was an old man, bent and bitter. His treasure had truly become a curse.

Lonely and tired, he sat down by the side of the road, his journey ending, and realised at last what the old woman had tried to tell him. This treasure truly held both a blessing and a curse. For all those wasted years, his hands had been fully occupied with holding on to something, and because this was all he valued, he could neither give nor receive. Because this was all he truly valued, this was all that he had. 'Perhaps,' he said to himself, 'if I'd taken the risk – put it down, shared it out – I might have been able to give and receive and live.'

And he finally found the courage to do what he should have done all those years before – he put the treasure down and walked away.

And the scene plays itself out over and over again. The treasure waits, biding its time, sparkling and shining until another young one comes down the road, so much like the ones we've all known: journey barely begun – potential and promise surrounding every step. When the treasure is found by the side of the road – beautiful and seductive, glistening as it catches the light – the reaction is exactly the same: *Who could ever leave behind something of this beauty? Who could put it aside – even for a moment?* And when the wise old one appears and offers hard-earned wisdom, he is, of course, not understood; the young are very young indeed.

It is said that as they walk away clasping their treasures to their chests, they oftentimes look back, just to make sure they aren't being followed, but see only a young one – carefree and happy – skipping across a field.

What do you value more than anything else? What do you hold close – what do you treasure? Consider this carefully ... because your heart and your treasure inevitably lie in the same place. And treasure truly does hold both a blessing and a curse. If your hands and heart are fully occupied with holding on to something, you can neither give nor receive. If there is something that keeps you held back, unable to follow the Christ who loves you, then put it down and walk away. Take the risk – put it down or share it out, give and receive and live.

What if? (meditation for an Advent service)

What if? What if we believed he was actually serious, not kidding, not exaggerating in the slightest when he said to share everything we have?

What if? What if our life was a gift to be given – what if we believed that nothing was ours to keep or hoard or hide, but only to share with the other people who share this planet.

What if? What if we learned the lesson of enough?

How many shoes can we wear?

How many clothes, toys, treats … do we need?

What if? What if what other people didn't have worried us more than what we wanted to get? What if we changed? Would it change things? We won't know unless we try.

And I'm not saying this because I want us to feel guilty about what we have – only aware … because we have some decisions to make every day. Will we share … or not?

What if, God? What if we shared our food? … Turn to a neighbour now and ask them what their favourite food is. Have a little chat about food and hunger in the world … So what if we saw food as a human right rather than as a commodity to be bought and sold to those who can afford it. What if?

Chant: 'God bless to us our bread', from *Love and Anger: Songs of Lively Faith and Social Justice*, John L. Bell and Graham Maule, Wild Goose Publications

What if, God? What if we shared our money. *(The leader empties his/her*

111

pockets and counts out how much money they are carrying, and then maybe asks a couple of other people in the congregation to do this too.) What if we saw our money as a common purse rather than as a personal allowance? What if?

Chant: 'God bless to us our bread'

What if, God? What if we shared our ideas and dreams? … You know we all have them … Take a moment to remember an idea or a dream you had. You don't have to say it out loud, but what if you did? What might happen? Who knows unless you give it a go! What if we thought of our ideas and dreams as neighbourhood ventures. What if?

Chant: 'God bless to us our bread'

What if? What if we believed he was actually serious, not kidding, not exaggerating in the slightest when he said to share everything we have?

What if? What if our life was a gift to be given – what if we believed that nothing was ours to keep or hoard or hide, but only to share with the other people who share this planet.

What if? What if we learned the lesson of enough?

Look around – at each other: you are looking at a gift – straight from God to you … Think about the ones you love – the ones who've created your centre, sculpted the beauty in you, helped you become, etched part of themselves into your hearts, written a chapter in your story … And think of the ones not here, but out there waiting for you to find them. They too are gifts straight from God … Treasure yet to be found, and you – treasure to them.

Look around – at each other: you are looking at a gift – straight from God.

ON PROPHETS AND HERALDS

Bible readings

Isaiah 40:1–11
Isaiah 61:1–4
Jeremiah 33:14–16
Joel 2:28–32
Matthew 5:11–12
Mark 1:1–8
John 1:19–28
1 John 4:1

The voices crying out – still

And still it shouts –
'the voice of one crying out in the wilderness' –
still calling:

in the refugee camp while factions feud;
in prisons where men and women sit in solid isolation and limbo
while life goes on outside;
in a home where they never feel safe;
in a village where there is too little food, too much disease,
and no oil or other bartering chip to bring the spotlight on them.

'Prepare the way of the Lord;
make his paths straight,' they cry.
'We're here,' they say.

But the news is more interested in who'll leave *Strictly*,
who'll win *The Voice* or *Britain's Got Talent*,
in 'how the economic downturn
is affecting sales on the High Street' …

God who hears the voice of the lonely and the desperate,
God who inspires their tenacious hope,
come among your people here
and unstop our ears.

If your way is to come,
then the path must be forged by us.

In this world where capitalism reigns and greed governs
and things are still ruled with iron fists guarding sealed vaults,
loosen our grip on the things that will not last,
but cause so much damage and oppression,
and help us to embrace your vision.

You have promised that every valley shall be filled:
help us to fill stomachs.
There is a vision of mountains and hills being made low:
teach us to level the playing field,
even if that means giving someone else a headstart.
You would have the crooked straightened
and the rough places made smooth:
if we deal crookedly and cause others to find their path rough,
bring us back
and head us in a different direction.

God, you pray that all flesh shall see your salvation;
in Christ, we learned that your salvation comes
when we are willing to participate in its advent.
Help us to herald your good tidings with our real repentance.
It's time to turn round and hear the voices crying out – still.
Amen

There is a voice crying out

There is a voice crying out ...
Whose will we hear calling in the wilderness?

God of love, let it be the voice of peace –
making straight our paths and giving us purpose;
clearing the rubble of anger and prejudice that keeps us stumbling;
building bridges of compassion
where we find ourselves cut off and bewildered;
finding ways to get through, to move beyond, to forge ahead.
Peace has a powerful voice –
let that be heard in the world's wilderness.

There is a voice crying out ...
Whose will we hear calling in the wilderness?

God of peace, let it be the voice of forgiveness –
gathering us gently in its arms,
washing us warmly in its calm,
holding us sacredly in its hopefulness.
Forgiveness has the sound of sense about it
in a world that so desperately needs to hear it.
May we open the ears of our hearts to her voice this day.

There is a voice crying out ...
Whose will we hear calling in the wilderness?

God of forgiveness, let it be the voice of justice –
asking awkward questions,
not taking no for an answer,

not being satisfied with lame excuses
and ineffectual mumblings.
Justice has the edge of persistence about it.
Keep it coming, because we have stubborn ears.

God, it is said that people are like grass:
they wither and fade –
'but your word will last forever'.
Help us remember to listen for your words:
'Love one another ... Forgive seventy times seven ...
Let justice roll down like waters.'

God, though we will all eventually wither and fade,
you pray for our time in the sun –
you are the feeder of flocks,
the gatherer of lambs;
you dream of carrying us gently in your arms.
Your voice comes speaking peace,
offering forgiveness,
demanding justice.
God, open us entirely that we may hear your voice
above it all.
Amen

ON CHRISTMAS EVE

Bible readings

Psalm 96
Isaiah 9:2–7
Matthew 1:18–2:12
Luke 2:1–20
Titus 2:11–14

Jesus, your birthday's almost here

Jesus, your birthday's almost here and it's getting dead exciting – we've got all the party decorations up, we've bought the presents, friends and family are winging or winding their way to us, or we're packing up getting ready to head out to them, and all the food – well, it's in the freezer and the fridge and falling out of the cupboards. And if we don't get too stuffed at the Guild Night out or the Sunday School party or the get-togethers at work or the special once-a-year hookups with friends before the big day, then we're sure to keep to tradition on Christmas Eve … Jesus, your birthday's almost here and it's getting dead exciting. Oh yeah, by the way – it *is* your birthday … feel free to drop by if you like. And since we've got presents for everybody else – is there anything we can get for you?

Reading: Matthew 25:34–40

Jesus, your birthday's almost here
and we're not in the least bit ready.
The party decorations are up,
but is there room and welcome in the inns of our hearts?

We've bought the presents,
but we still hide and hoard our gifts.

Friends and family are winging or winding their way to us,
or we're packing up getting ready to head out to them,
but so many of our family in you still cry out in despair,
because they don't have any homes at all.

And the food –
well, it's in our freezers and our fridges

and falling out of our cupboards,
not to mention our rubbish bins,
while other people actually starve.

Jesus, your birthday's almost here
and we're not in the least bit ready ...

Forgive us for forgetting
the real tradition established by your birth:
the amazing gift that was given in a tiny, fragile,
vulnerable infant
who taught us that to give our all
to those who have least
is the best gift we could ever give to you or to ourselves ...

Jesus, your birthday's almost here –
don't just drop by:
be born in us again.
Set up residence,
settle down
and move us over.
And since we've left so many you love off our Christmas lists,
help us to find a gift for them.

A story that quickens the heart

On the hillsides,
hope was heard singing unexpected Hallelujahs.
In a Bethlehem backwater,
hope hovered
and love was born.
And now,
as the wise journey and the powerful start to pace the floor
and mumble into sleepless nights,
we gather –
the light of the world is here.
The job now is to keep it burning.

'Gloria, Gloria, Gloria'

For crisp, clear, frost-etched winter days that wake us up
to your artistic flare;
for the stirring of life even in the deepest, darkest day;
for wee acts of love that lift our spirits
and send us scurrying back to hope,
thank you, God.
Glory to you …

Chant: a 'Gloria' (e.g. 'Iona Gloria', CH4)

For the people who pack the malls,
who trudge the streets,
who lug packages
and place them precariously on bus seats
and train-overheads;
for older people who smile at children –
and for children who shout and sing to everybody
and infect them with the Christmas spirit;
for parents who meet themselves coming and going –
who pray that Santa will bring toys already assembled,
because the gifts they've bought come in a gazillion pieces
and can't be put together until Christmas Eve –
for the joy of this crazy season, glory to you.

Chant

But wake us up, God,
to the *essence* of Christmas,
to the needs of a world
desperate for wee acts of love
that might herald a change;
wake us up God,
to the things we do unthinkingly
that make life harder for those who already struggle
and for those yet to come.
Wake us up
and call us to care enough to be different.

If we will sing glory to you in the highest,
then we have to hear your story:
where the peaceful rule,
where the poor come first,
where all cluster round your cradle
and there is room.
So be with all who need you;
send us to all the places where we can help;
change our ways.

Glory to you ...

Chant

Amen

Christmas Eve call to be together

Leader: Children, turn to the nearest grown-up and, on the count of three, whisper: 'It's time.' … 1, 2, 3 …

Grown-ups, turn to the nearest child and, on the count of three, whisper: 'I know.' … 1, 2, 3 …

This is the night when the star shone overhead and the angels sang their song. This is the night when the shepherds left their fields in search of the most precious lamb, and this is the night when the wise set off on a journey that would take them home a different way. This is the night when a baby drew his first breath and then breathed peace on everyone and everything he met – even to today.

Open the eyes of your heart, look heavenward and expect the star. It's time, you know.

The 'Come On Inn'

(Setting: outside the inn)

Person 1:   All these unacceptable folk – God! Did you get a load of that pregnant, unmarried girl and her 'husband-to-be'? Now, I'm not one for gossip, but I've heard rumours they're not exactly sure who the real father is, but there he is – right there with her, all proud, acting like the doting dad. If they had any money, he'd probably be handing out cigars! Ridiculous – ought to be embarrassed, but he doesn't even have enough sense to know that.

Person 2:   He's either a wimp or an idiot or both … Well, at least they're out back away from the paying customers. Did you see the riff-raff that came to see them? I cannot imagine the uproar and complaints if they'd traipsed through the lobby.

Person 1:   What, those dirty shepherd types? You just can't trust them – I can't believe that girl let them near that baby. Think of all the germs they probably hauled in with them. But who cares anyway? She's probably not got the sense God gave her.

Person 2:   True, but there is something just downright strange about all of this. Now, as you know, I'm not one for gossip, but I heard a rumour that there are some foreigners coming here who actually claim that that baby is a king. That baby is a nobody, but you know how ignorant foreigners can be.

Person 1:   Well, you know what else that could be, don't you? That's probably some enemy terrorist plot to undermine the government's authority – to divide us against each other. You know what those people are like. You've got to watch out, stick with your own. I mean, for heaven's sake, what would *they* know about *our* king? What would they know about anything!

Person 2:   I know, all these unacceptable folk – God! If they weren't so insignificant, I'd say they were asking for trouble. It's a dangerous thing to claim that some fatherless baby is a king. You don't want to get on the wrong side of the right people.

Person 1:   Yeah, but they've probably not got the sense God gave them, and at least they're out back and not on the inside like the rest of us.

Reading: Matthew 25:31–40

(Setting: outside the church)

Person 1:   Well, you'd know it was Christmas again, even if there weren't any of those blow-up snow globes and 8-foot Rudolphs in the gardens. They're coming out of the flippin' woodwork – clanging bells outside Sainsbury's and M&S, ringing my doorbell and asking for donations for everything from Christian Aid to the dog and cat home! And folk keep dragging in here too – needing help with this and money for that. If they couldn't afford all those kids, then they shouldn't have had them. Christmas morning doesn't come cheap!

Person 2:   Speaking of Christmas morning, do you know that the wife signed me up to cook turkeys for the shelter again – does she not understand that Christmas is a time for SKY sports and naps? I don't want to spend my holiday getting burned by turkey fat, or even worse, getting a blister on my thumb from that stupid potato peeler. I think it would make a lot more sense to do this big 'feed the hungry' dinner some other time. You know – sometime more convenient – when we're all not so busy.

Person 1: Speaking of busy and coming out of the woodwork – the minister asked me to be a greeter on Christmas Eve this year. And it will be almost impossible to park – all these folk who make a special guest appearance on Christmas Eve and Easter morning should be ashamed of themselves – the least they could do is park down the street a bit. If they're only going to come to church twice a year, then they can afford a little hike to get there. It might even work off some of that Christmas cheer they've piled on at their office parties. You know, I think I'll recommend to the Kirk Session next year that we have 'members only' parking reserved for the legitimate worshippers.

Person 2: Yeah, there was even talk this year about having one service with all the Churches together! Some new-fangled idea about being ecumenical/all the Churches working together ... There's even talk of working with other faiths in town, like the Jews and the Methodists. Why, if we do that, then pretty soon, we'd all be alike – like one big family or something – *then* where would we be?

ON CHRISTMAS MORNING

Bible readings

Isaiah 9:6–7
Isaiah 40:9
Luke 2:14
John 3:16
Titus 3:4–7
Hebrews 1:1–2

On Christmas morning!

It's just gone 10:30 in the morning, God,
but some of us have been up since the crack of dawn …
Excitement is not a sleep-inducing essence.
Santa's come and gone –
he's such a good guy, one of your really best ideas.
Our living room's strewn with paper,
the turkey's on,
and Uncle Oscar from Auchtermuchty
is having a long lie in our guest room.
Christmas.

Thank you for all you've given us;
not the stuff but the people:
their love,
their dreams,
the possibilities that weave their way
into our days.
Christmas.

Tell us …
tell us again about forgiveness that frees,
about love that is boundless,
about peace that passes all understanding.

Christmas –
the gift of you that introduces us
to each other.
Amen

ON THE STORY

Bible readings

Psalm 19:14
Psalm 119:105
Proverbs 16:24
Matthew 4:4
John 1:1

I don't know if it happened exactly this way, but ...'

The birth of Jesus. Since probably before you knew what you were hearing, you've heard this story. Hopefully it's done what all good stories do – it's gone deep: past your ears and your head, lodged firmly in your heart and maybe even deeper – embedded itself somewhere in the core of your being – that's where changes come from ...

A Native American storyteller begins all his stories with the phrase: *'I don't know if it happened exactly this way, but I know this story to be true.'*[1] We people of the post-modern age have an important hurdle to get over if we are to understand the power of this gift we've been given – because this most sacred of stories is a gift, make no mistake. It has the power to make people lay down their weapons – if only for a day. I'm thinking about the German and British soldiers in the First World War trenches, who laid down their killing machines to play football with each other on Christmas Day. It has the power to change preconceived notions and stubborn hearts, to open pockets and minds long closed. There is a profound truth in the story of Jesus' coming: a message of peace on earth, goodwill to all. But we have to remember that being factual and being true don't mean the same thing. So let's consider what we might hear and understand if we began our story with: *'I don't know if it happened exactly this way, but I know this story to be true.'*

What might we make of Mary?: a frightened, insignificant girl who had the audacity to believe *'nothing will be impossible with God'* – that the whole world might be delivered through her 'Yes'; someone who was willing to risk her reputation, her future, her everything because God asked her to.

What might we understand of her virginity?: not some essential divine attribute because human beings are somehow unworthy; the virgin birth not some unbelievable happening that we must accept without question if we are to remain within the faith – but a beautiful metaphorical expression by the authors of these stories. 'We have seen the face of God in this man, Jesus.'

What could we glean from the star and the wise men, if we were not tied to trying to explain this phenomenon rationally: a star that freely roams across the sky, actually turning left and stopping over an exact spot – as if directed by some ancient form of GPS or satnav. What if the story tells us about a light in the deepest darkness, leading us to a love so pure that it sends us home by another path – changed forever by what we experienced; unable to go back to what we saw before as powerful, because everything we used to understand about power has been turned on its head?

And what of the shepherds and the angels? Maybe God comes to the poorest first – good news for them at last? The wise travel and journey to God, but God finds the poor where they are and whispers first to them that justice is coming.

'I don't know if it happened exactly this way, but I know this story to be true.' So what will you make of this ancient story? The one you've probably heard before you knew what you were hearing, the one that's hopefully done what all good stories do: gone deep, past your ears and your head, lodged firmly in your heart and maybe even deeper – embedded itself somewhere in the core of your being – that's where changes come from.

What kind of impact could this kind of understanding and seeing make on us listening today? Well, when we're asked to say 'Yes' in the face of daunting odds and big risk, will the story speak its wisdom? When we think we glimpse the face of God in the face of a stranger, will we take a closer look? When money and power and staying safe and secure seem like the sensible focus for our lives, will we be able to see light in our darkness, and turn and walk another way? The story is a gift, to make of what we will. So what will you make of it this year?

1. Quoted in *Reading the Bible Again for the First Time: Taking the Bible seriously but not literally*, Marcus J. Borg, HarperCollins, 2001

Sources and acknowledgements

Some of the pieces in this book were first published in the periodical *The Expository Times:* http://ext.sagepub.com/

Bible passages used throughout from the NRSV. New Revised Standard Version Bible, copyright 1989, Division of Christian Education of the National Council of the Churches of Christ in the United States of America. Used by permission. All rights reserved.

Wild Goose Publications is part of the Iona Community, which is:

- An ecumenical movement of men and women from different walks of life and different traditions in the Christian church
- Committed to the gospel of Jesus Christ, and to following where that leads, even into the unknown
- Engaged together, and with people of goodwill across the world, in acting, reflecting and praying for justice, peace and the integrity of creation
- Convinced that the inclusive community we seek must be embodied in the community we practise

Together with our staff, we are responsible for:

- Our islands residential centres of Iona Abbey, the MacLeod Centre on Iona, and Camas Adventure Centre on the Ross of Mull

and in Glasgow:

- The administration of the Community
- Our work with young people
- Our publishing house, Wild Goose Publications
- Our association in the revitalising of worship with the Wild Goose Resource Group

The Iona Community was founded in Glasgow in 1938 by George MacLeod, minister, visionary and prophetic witness for peace, in the context of the poverty and despair of the Depression. Its original task of rebuilding the monastic ruins of Iona Abbey became a sign of hopeful rebuilding of community in Scotland and beyond. Today, we are about 250 Members, mostly in Britain, and 1500 Associate Members, with 1400 Friends worldwide. Together and apart, 'we follow the light we have, and pray for more light'.

For information on the Iona Community contact:
The Iona Community, Fourth Floor, Savoy House, 140 Sauchiehall Street,
Glasgow G2 3DH, UK. Phone: 0141 332 6343
admin@iona.org.uk   www.iona.org.uk

For enquiries about visiting Iona, please contact:
Iona Abbey, Isle of Iona, Argyll PA76 6SN, UK. Phone: 01681 700404
ionacomm@iona.org.uk